Early Childhood, After School, and Youth Program Administrator Competencies and Self-Assessment Tool

Angel Stoddard, MS

Pam Boulton, Ed.D

ISBN – 13: 978-1981888528

ISBN – 10: 1981888527

Contents

Overview

The field of early childhood, after school and youth programming (EC/AS/YP) is all about relationships! The administrator sets the tone, creates the climate and models the behaviors, skills and dispositions they want others to embrace. They do this most successfully through relationships with staff, children and families, and colleagues.

Our goal is to articulate the many facets of the role of administrator and the variety of knowledge, skills and dispositions needed to be successful managers and leaders. We acknowledge that leadership is the bigger umbrella that carries all these competencies. Gwen Morgan writes that the *"director is the key to quality"* in any early childhood [and after school or youth] program. That is a powerful statement. Her work outlines an ecological perspective where we draw best practices from business, education, social work, psychology, sociology, and health care. This multifaceted perspective results in layers of ethical dilemmas the administrator must address regularly. We know an administrator must be able to fluidly move in and out of these intersecting but differing interests and needs. We hope these competencies create a common language for administrators to articulate and advocate for the workload and heavy responsibilities they carry.

According to Barbara Daley (1999), professionals move through a developmental continuum in which they progress from novice to expert. Dreyfus and Dreyfus (1995) identify professionals as moving through five stages of career development: novice, advanced beginner, competent, proficient, and expert. It is our hope that administrators use these competencies and the self-assessment as a tool to intentionally plan for their ongoing professional development. To that end, we have provided an outline of what the developmental continuum might look like for early childhood, after school and youth program administrators.

According to Merriam-Webster online dictionary, being competent is "the ability to do something successfully or efficiently." Therefore, these competencies are a list of what an administrator should know and be able to do successfully.

> "Director, know thyself!"
>
> -unknown

Format

The Early Childhood, After School and Youth Program Administrator Competencies are intended to be comprehensive, although not exhaustive, providing specific guidance for best practices when leading and managing a program.

Core Area (1, 2, 3, 4)

Competency (A, B, C...)

Indicator

*Note: the indictors are not in a hierarchical order, meaning one is not more important than another.

1. Dispositions (symbol: Mobius strip/infinity circle)

   A. Self-Management

   B. Relationship Management

2. Operations Management (symbol: key)

   A. Regulatory Compliance

   B. Business Practices

   C. Financial Management and Planning

   D. Marketing and Public Relations

   E. Human Resources and Talent Management

3. Programming for Children and Families (symbol: sprout)

   A. Workforce Development

   B. Assessment

   C. Curriculum Design and Implementation

   D. Family and Community Engagement

4. Influential Leadership (symbol: flame)

   A. Shared Vision

   B. Culture and Climate

   C. Advocacy

Graphic Image

The graphic of gears visually references the complexity of the role of an administrator while also showing that everything is connected; and that making a change in one competency will impact the other competencies.

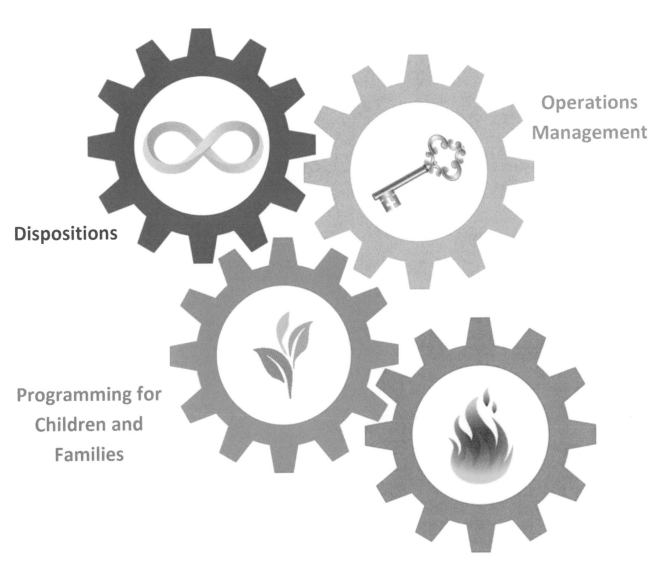

Dispositions

Operations Management

Programming for Children and Families

Influential Leadership

Purpose

Pam Boulton (2008), explains that the administrator, "is responsible for every aspect of the program. What emerges is the picture of a complex job with an overlay of day-to-day detail, and a need to communicate and collaborate at every level with clarity and precision. The role is multi-faceted, ranging from basic sanitation to educational, fiscal, and legal responsibilities with far-reaching implications. It requires skill in communication, decision making, resource management, and leadership." She concludes by noting that administrators, "feel the weight of the field on their shoulders."

We recognize that wherever an administrator may begin to look at this role, there are multiple layers to every aspect, leading to a role that can be overwhelming at times.

These competencies provide a framework that makes the role of an administrator accessible. We know the few begin with a deep and wide understanding of the role of the leader/manager. To support quality outcomes for children, families and communities, administrators need to demonstrate an understanding of the systems, policies, research and agency collaborations that support diverse programs, locally and nationally.

These competencies will inform stakeholders with an understanding that the administrator is the key to quality in any early childhood, after school, or youth program.

The McCormick Center for Early Childhood Leadership's (2014) research states, "There is a positive relationship between the quality of administrative practices and the quality of the children's learning environment in center based programs."

In part, these competencies are a response to the Institute of Medicine's Report (2015), Transforming the Workforce for Children Birth Through Age 8 which notes, "The complexity of childhood development and early learning and the sophisticated knowledge and competencies needed by care and education professionals have important implications for the knowledge and competencies of leadership in settings for children from birth through age 8."

These competencies complement those for educators by acknowledging that all administrators must have a working knowledge and understanding of what practitioners should know and be able to do that lead to successful outcomes for young children. In addition, administrators must have a thorough understanding of learning standards. For this reason, we have developed a self-assessment tool for administrators to use to consider their strengths and areas for future growth.

Finally, these competencies will create a common thread of professional development expectations across the variety of system partners (Institutions of Higher Education, Head Start, Department of Education, State Department's for Children and Families, Quality Rating Systems, and professional organizations).

Uses

The Administrator Competencies have been designed as a framework that complements other professional development systems. Below are some examples of how they might be used:

Framework

- To support career pathways
- To inform professional development opportunities that support administrators
- For Institutions of Higher Education to support students

Guidance

- For networking
- For evidence-based and high-quality practices in programs

Resource

- For individuals to inform their work
- For programs to write position descriptions
- For programs hiring new administrators
- For professional development and continuing education
- To Institutions of Higher Education who provide credentials or certificates for administrators

Definitions

While these definitions provide some guidance for the information outlined in these competencies, the list is not all-inclusive and some individuals may have similar or different titles yet do the work of any position listed below. For the purposes of this document, we will refer to "Administrator" to mean any one of the titles below or any title that fits any of these responsibilities.

In any program, there may be one person who does these things, or there may be more than one person and they may have differentiated duties. These are 'jobs titles/responsibilities' not people.

Administrator: Responsibility for the overall business both through leadership and management. This individual's role relates to comprehensive planning to help the program clarify and affirm vision and mission through the development and implementation of a strategic plan.

Center Director: Responsibility for the managerial components of the business through the development and implementation of systems, policies and procedures that support the vision and mission.

Program Coordinator: Responsibility for the educational programming including curriculum, child assessment, and inclusive practices.

Operations Manager: Responsibility for the daily operations of the facilities.

Supervisor (Site Supervisor): Responsibility for the supervision of staff to ensure compliance with rules and regulations as well as program policies.

And there are likely other positions/titles.

Directions for Individual Use of the Self-Assessment Tool

These 14 competencies can stand alone to inform the scope of the role of an administrator. However, an administrator can also use these competencies for self-assessment, to determine which areas/competencies are a strength and which show a need for growth.

First, review the Skill Acquisition – Stages of Development found on pages 10-11 to gain an understanding of the characteristics/descriptions of each stage (Beginner – Expert). For professional honesty and consistency, reflect on the last 6 months of your work habits rather than on your whole professional career.

Next, for each Core Area that fits within your position responsibilities review the indicators under each Competency. Reflect on your level of competence in each and write either 1 (Beginner), 2 (Developing), 3 (Proficient) or 4 (Expert) on the line in front of each indicator.

> For example, looking at Core Area 1. Dispositions, under the competency of Self-Management, how competent are you in making "large and small decision with thoughtful intentionality by considering all perspectives"? Remember to look back only over the previous 6 months, not your whole career. Ask yourself, "How well do I do this now?" Then put a 1, 2, 3, or 4 depending on your skill acquisition/stage of development.

Using your professional judgment, determine which Stage (Beginner – Expert) best reflects each indicator and write the corresponding number on each line.

Next, add up the numbers under each competency and divide by the total number in that section. Transfer that number to the bar graph near the end of this booklet.

Complete the bar graph by coloring in or drawing a line to the determined stage. The horizontal dotted line allows you to complete the Inventory twice, consider every 6 months or yearly to ensure continuous quality improvement.

Finally, complete the Action Plan on page 30.

Skill Acquisition – Stages of Development

Dreyfus & Dreyfus' framework for skill acquisition (1980), and Daley's (1999) work on how professionals learn through a developmental continuum were the primary resources used to outline the stages administrators may go through as they develop the skills, knowledge and dispositions of a highly effective leader and manager. This can be seen as a continuum where unfamiliar information may result in the administrator going back to the novice stage while acquiring new knowledge, which can happen any time new policies or mandates are enacted. A few examples are provided to help readers understand each stage.

1. Beginner – (comprehension/understanding) manage and lead the program by adhering to laws and policies

> Communicates basic understanding of child development

> Develops knowledge, skills and dispositions to support the program

> Maintains daily operations

> Provides supervision to staff

> Recognizes situations recurring in similar circumstances

> Seeks support from others when challenges arise

> Understands meaning of regulations and policies

2. Developing – (application) manages and leads the program with increasing independence and effectiveness

> Ensures effectiveness and efficiency of daily operations

Has emerging knowledge of best practices in early childhood and youth theories

Has knowledge, skills and dispositions to modify program components

Makes decisions consistent with program mission and philosophy

3. Proficient – (analysis & synthesis) manages and leads the program with independence, efficiency and effectiveness

Assimilates current research about evidence-based practice and guides others toward more effective practice

Assimilates knowledge, skills and dispositions to plan program components grounded in best practice

Engages in discussions around child development, program policies, and regulatory laws, applying rationale and concrete examples to increase knowledge and understanding of others

Establishes systems for ongoing evaluation across programming; routinely involves others in decision-making

Makes decisions consistent with program vision

Recognizes the importance of feedback, assessment, planning and modification to effectively oversee the program

Supports others to ensure clear oral and written communication; recognizes the need to solicit advice to those with expertise to ensure effective communication

4. Expert - (evaluation/creating) manage and support the program by providing strong leadership and high-quality program components that promote the well-being of staff, children and families.

Aligns vision and mission with the needs of the community, and ensures program is consistent with current research and learning standards.

Aligns program components with advances in theory and evidence-based practices

Assimilates deep knowledge, skills, and dispositions across competency areas and uses this knowledge to define and shape the mission, vision, and philosophy

Embodies strong leadership skills and leverages these skills to advance the program

Provides guidance and training to others to help build the capacity of the EC/AS/YP field in their community/state.

Core Area 1: Dispositions

These indicators are ESSENTIAL and can be learned through intentionality and self-reflection. According to Daniel Goleman (2014), emotional intelligence is our keystone to administration, program development and leadership.

Self-Management

____ Ability to make large and small decisions with thoughtful intentionality by considering all perspectives

____ Demonstrates compassion toward self and others

____ Exhibits confidence in one's own abilities

____ Values a continuous improvement mindset for self

____ Understands cultural awareness in all relationships

____ Maintains a high level of ethical behavior with awareness of Codes of Conduct

____ Displays humility and integrity

____ Is open and willing to explore innovative ideas when seeking solutions

____ Shows passion for field/work through professional action and words

____ Can persevere through troublesome situations

____ Can solve immediate, short-term, and long-term problems or dilemmas

____ Models professionalism

____ Incorporates reflective practice as a routine part of the work

____ Is reliable in deed and word

____ Shows resiliency and responsibility

____ Is willing to take appropriate risks

____ Exhibits self-awareness and how their behavior impacts others

____ Ability to manage time for planning specific to quality improvement

____ Values humor

Add up all the numbers _____

Divide that by 19 (the number of indicators in this competency)

Equals your average stage of development for this competency. _____

Transfer this number to the bar graph on the Self-Assessment on page 30.

Relationship Management

___ Exhibits empathy and compassion with others

___ Communicates effectively to ensure continued positive relationships using a variety of strategies

___ Seeks to understand others with open-mindedness

___ Ability to manage conflict while maintaining focus on resolution

___ Builds positive relationships through supportive respect for others

___ Understands generational and cultural influences that impact relationships

___ Encourages a collaborative climate within professional relationships

___ Facilitates effective group processes (conflict resolution, problem solving, goal setting)

___ Has capacity to remain mindfully present

___ Focuses on strength of self and others

___ Values shared power

___ Has an awareness of social justice issues

___ Builds capacity of others through strategies such as empowerment and delegation

___ Establishes ethical boundaries with stakeholders

Self-Assessment Scoring

Add up all the numbers _____

Divide that by 14 (the number of indicators in this competency)

Equals your average stage of development for this competency. _____

Transfer this number to the bar graph on the Self-Assessment on page 30.

Core Area 2: Operations Management

These indicators address the extensive knowledge of business best practices, as well as thorough knowledge of the laws and regulations applicable to their program. Early Childhood, After School and Youth Development programs are bound by numerous laws, regulations, and policies originating across multiple agencies and levels of government. Adherence to these requirements is central to the role of the administrator. Maintenance and enhancement of the facility requires knowledge of local/state/federal codes; as well as financial planning. These competencies address the core knowledge and skills needed to effectively operate a fiscally sound program, including the ability to increase enrollment.

Regulatory Compliance

___ Demonstrates knowledge of and enforcement of regulations: local ordinances and licensing, Federal and State Labor Laws, OSHA, Federal and State Unemployment laws, Workers' Compensation, Equal Opportunity, and proper hiring/termination and discrimination rules

___ Understands and plans for risk management and assessment

___ Implements policies and procedures for other requirements such as Child and Adult Care Food Program and accreditation

___ Understands insurance requirements and liabilities for the business

Self-Assessment Scoring

Add up all the numbers _____

Divide that by 4 (the number of indicators in this competency)

Equals your average stage of development for this competency. _____

Transfer this number to the bar graph on the Self-Assessment on page 30.

Business Practices (internal, specific to EC/AS/YP)

___ Ability to create and enforce program policies, standard operating procedures

___ Exhibits ability to manage simple and complex tasks

___ Develops and implements systems to ensure smooth operations within and between all components of the business

___ Exhibits skills in management of indoor and outdoor facilities, and program and classrooms resources

___ Exhibits ability to manage time for self and others

___ Understands general knowledge of business planning including the business status of the program (for-profit, government, etc.)

___ Has working knowledge of current technologies that support the running of the center

___ Shows an awareness of current trends in the field of business, management and leadership

___ Ability to create, implement, and track reports as necessary

Self-Assessment Scoring

Add up all the numbers _____

Divide that by 9 (the number of indicators in this competency)

Equals your average stage of development for this competency. _____

Transfer this number to the bar graph on the Self-Assessment on page 30.

Financial Management and Planning

___ Understands payroll practices including taxes, benefits, FICA, etc.

___ Demonstrates ability to develop a fiscal budget, with monthly monitoring

___ Develops and oversees contracts, MOUs, etc.

___ Demonstrates knowledge of short and long-term fiscal planning

___ Understands and creates a breakeven analysis

___ Exhibits an understanding and control of cash flow

___ Understands and explains a Profit/Loss statement

___ Has basic knowledge of fundraising

___ Has basic knowledge of grant writing

___ Can forecast short and long-range influences/trends that impact and/or shape the current and future business

___ Understands, plans, and manages risk mitigation and associated costs

___ Identifies, understands, and manages cost drivers and variable costs

Self-Assessment Scoring

Add up all the numbers _____

Divide that by 12 (the number of indicators in this competency)

Equals your average stage of development for this competency. _____

Transfer this number to the bar graph on the Self-Assessment on page 30.

Marketing and Public Relations

___ Understands general marketing strategies

___ Utilizes social media to support program stability/growth

___ Articulates the philosophy, vision and mission of the program

___ Embraces and champions the center's philosophy, vision, and its uniqueness to all stakeholders

___ Understands and identifies internal and external stakeholders

___ Gathers and analyzes community data that directly and indirectly impacts the program

___ Develops a community needs assessment as necessary

___ Defines and refines the center's market branding philosophy

Self-Assessment Scoring

Add up all the numbers _____

Divide that by 8 (the number of indicators in this competency)

Equals your average stage of development for this competency. _____

Transfer this number to the bar graph on the Self-Assessment on page 30.

____ Supervises staff

____ Implements strategies for recruitment and retention of qualified staff

____ Maintains a healthy and safe environment for staff

____ Ensures the implementation of an accepted Code of Conduct

____ Understands and advocates for staff benefits

____ Regularly includes staff in operational planning and design

Self-Assessment Scoring

Add up all the numbers _____

Divide that by 6 (the number of indicators in this competency)

Equals your average stage of development for this competency. _____

Transfer this number to the bar graph on the Self-Assessment on page 30.

Core Area 3: Programming for Children and Families

These indicators address the core knowledge and skills needed to ensure the development of relationships and collaborations with families and the community that support and promote the needs of the children. Highly motivated and effective staff are central to the daily experiences of children and families. Effective administrators have extensive knowledge of child growth and development and early learning guidelines that support their ability to select appropriate curriculum, support staff, and communicate it to staff and families.

Workforce Development

___ Has knowledge of best practices for teaching, mentoring and coaching adults

___ Keeps current on trends/research related to child and youth development such as brain research, curriculum, etc.

___ Provides instructional leadership as content and curriculum specialist

___ Displays skills in supporting staff to implement best practices based on current trends/research

___ Understands and can support staff to ensure developmentally appropriate teaching

___ Ensures appropriate Inclusive practices through continuous support of staff

___ Values reflective supervision

___ Understands the process of and implements effective staff development

___ Builds a diverse team that is strength-based

___ Supports staff to enhance their own self and cultural awareness

___ Creates and executes employee evaluations, review, and reward process, including professional development and training

___ Regularly includes staff in operational planning and design

Self-Assessment Scoring

Add up all the numbers _____

Divide that by 12 (the number of indicators in this competency)

Equals your average stage of development for this competency. _____

Transfer this number to the bar graph on the Self-Assessment on page 30.

Assessment

____ Implements a comprehensive program assessment

____ Connects current trends/research with assessment of children

____ Uses available data from a variety of assessment tools to inform practice

____ Supports staff in the use of an evidence-based assessment tool

____ Implements an ongoing formal and informal strategy to evaluate staff

____ Supports staff in designing, implementing and maintaining high quality environments for children, both inside and outside, using evidence-based assessments

____ Supports staff in implementing developmental screenings

____ Understands the value of including families in the screening and assessment of children

____ Supports staff in the development and design of portfolios and other tools that show growth over time

____ Understands how technology can support assessment

Self-Assessment Scoring

Add up all the numbers _____

Divide that by 10 (the number of indicators in this competency)

Equals your average stage of development for this competency. _____

Transfer this number to the bar graph on the Self-Assessment on page 30.

Curriculum Design and Implementation

____ Has deep knowledge of child and/or youth development

____ Exhibits fidelity to curriculum philosophy

____ Ensures curriculum includes 5 Developmental Domains (Health and Physical; Social and

Emotional; Language and Communication; Cognition and General Knowledge; Approaches

to Learning) appropriate for each age group (WMELS, 2014)

____ Reflects upon current trends/research and its impact on curriculum/daily scheduling

____ Ensures curriculum is anchored with research and grounded in Developmentally Appropriate

Practice (Copple & Bredekamp, 2009)

____ Understands the importance of the environment both inside and outside

____ Ensures curriculum reflects diversity and inclusion

Self-Assessment Scoring

Add up all the numbers _____

Divide that by 7 (the number of indicators in this competency)

Equals your average stage of development for this competency. _____

Transfer this number to the bar graph on the Self-Assessment on page 30.

Family and Community Engagement

____ Communicates with families on an ongoing basis

____ Supports teachers' skill development in both informal and formal communication with
families

____ Ensures Parent-Teacher Conferences are respectful and valuable

____ Effectively communicates vision, mission, goals, curriculum and outcomes to families and

community

Self-Assessment Scoring

Add up all the numbers _____

Divide that by 4 (the number of indicators in this competency)

Equals your average stage of development for this competency. _____

Transfer this number to the bar graph on the Self-Assessment on page 30.

Core Area 4: Influential Leadership

Early childhood, After School and Youth Program leaders serve a valuable and complex role, that in part, ensures the use of ethical guidelines and other professional standards related to practice. These indicators address creating a culture of continuous quality improvement through a shared vision. This section captures the advocacy role leaders play in the EC/AS/YP field.

Shared Vision

___ Mobilizes people toward effective collaboration

___ Establishes shared importance of continuous quality improvement and goal setting

___ Builds consensus with multiple stakeholders coming to agreement

___ Exhibits fidelity to the vision and mission of the program

___ Articulates and acts with passion and purpose

___ Holds a professional philosophy toward excellence

___ Understands the value of transparency in all aspects of the program

___ Inspires others around a shared vision

___ Demonstrates skills in strategic thinking and planning

___ Values diversity that is reflected in the vision, mission and throughout the program

___ Provides direction, trust and hope to staff and families

___ Empowers others through delegation

___ Shares successes and processes within the EC/AS/YP community

Self-Assessment Scoring

Add up all the numbers _____

Divide that by 13 (the number of indicators in this competency)

Equals your average stage of development for this competency. _____

Transfer this number to the bar graph on the Self-Assessment on page 30.

Culture and Climate

___ Establishes and cultivates relationships with families, staff, and stakeholders within the community

___ Creates an environment to meet the needs of adults

___ Inspires a culture of excellence through quality improvement practices

___ Focuses on family and community partnerships

___ Encourages everyone to embrace a learning organization atmosphere

___ Thinks systemically, understanding that everything is connected

___ Acts as a role model and mentor to create a supportive staff culture

___ Includes staff in planning and design

Self-Assessment Scoring

Add up all the numbers _____

Divide that by 8 (the number of indicators in this competency)

Equals your average stage of development for this competency. _____

Transfer this number to the bar graph on the Self-Assessment on page 30.

Advocacy

___ Is aware of external trends including both opportunities and threats that impact the program

___ Is a change agent, advocating for children and families and staff

___ Brings key stakeholders together to coordinate advocacy efforts

___ Identifies allies

___ Is active in administrator networks/communities of practice and professional organizations

___ Understands and stays informed of political implications on a local, state and national level

___ Understands that transparency supports advocacy

Self-Assessment Scoring

Add up all the numbers _____

Divide that by 7 (the number of indicators in this competency)

Equals your average stage of development for this competency. _____

Transfer this number to the bar graph on the Self-Assessment on page 30.

About the Lead Authors

Angel Stoddard, MS

Educator, trainer, author, coach, innovator, leader, learner. These are a few roles Angel has played (never seen as work) in her 25-year career. Angel's mission each day is to show up (stand up, step in, sit down, lean in) with passion and purpose, with curiosity and courage. She is driven to elevate the role leader's hold in ensuring quality programming, as evidenced by these competencies. In her role as full-time instructor for the University of Wisconsin – Milwaukee's Center for Early Childhood Professional Development and Leadership, Angel designs, develops and presents professional development opportunities for local, state and national audiences. Angel is driven by a deep belief that leaders must be learners and aims to inspire the joy of learning in others. Email at ajs21@uwm.edu

Pam Boulton, Ed.D

Pam is Child Care Director Emeritus after her 40-year tenure as the Director of the UW-Milwaukee Children's Center. She currently serves as the Coordinator for the Exchange Leadership Initiative for Exchange Magazine and is an Instructor for the Center for Early Childhood Professional Development and Leadership in the UW-Milwaukee School of Continuing Education. She is actively involved in the Wisconsin Nature Action Collaborative for Children. Pam continues to be a guiding force in the design, development and delivery of child care leadership courses, training programs and professional development opportunities at the local, state and national level. Email at boulton@uwm.edu

Contributors

Chanel Clark, Director: Little Chicks Learning Academy, Madison
Verna Drake, Owner/Administrator: Westby Day Care & Learning Center, Westby
Maria Fitz-Gibbon, Administrator: Leap Academy Child Development Center, Waunakee
Denise Green, Director: La Causa Early Education & Care Center, Milwaukee
April Greenman, Senior Director of School Age Education: YMCA of Metropolitan Milwaukee
Julie Schroeder, Co-Director: Christian Community Child Center-7th Avenue, Oshkosh
Michael Siegler: Owner/Administrator: Happy Hollow Learning Center, Hartford
Cigdem Unal, Director: Campus Child Care and Family Resources, University of Wisconsin: Madison
Content also reviewed by 75 attendees from the Wisconsin Child Care Administrator's State Pre-Conference, 2017. Input also given by students in the Wisconsin Administrator Credential Fall 2017 courses at University of Wisconsin - Milwaukee.

Resources

Abel, M., Talan, T., & Masterson, M. (2017) Whole Leadership: A Framework for Early Childhood Programs – retrieved from: http://mccormickcenter.nl.edu/whole-leadership-a-framework-for-early-childhood-programs/

Bennis, W. (2009) *On becoming a leader* Philadelphia, PA. Perseus Books Group.

Boulton, Pam (Jan-Feb, 2008). The Child Care Director: Not Just Anyone Can Do This Job! *Exchange: The Early Childhood Leaders' Magazine.* 179 (16-19)

Brown, K., Squires, J., Connors-Tadros, L., & Horowitz, M., (July, 2014) What Do We Know About Principal Preparation, Licensure Requirements, and Professional Development for School Leaders?; CEELO Policy Report – retrieved from: http://ceelo.org/wp-content/uploads/2014/07/ceelo_policy_report_ece_principal_prep.pdf

Copple, C., and Bredekamp, S. (2009). Developmentally Appropriate Practice in Early Childhood Programs, 3rd Edition. Washington, DC: National Association for the Education of Young Children.

Daley, B. (1999). Novice to Expert: An Exploration of How Professionals Learn. *Adult Education Quarterly*, 49(4), 133-146. Doi: 10.1177/07417136990400401

Dreyfus, S.E.; & Dreyfus, H.L. (1980) *A Five-stage Model of Mental Activities Involved in Directed Skill Acquisition.* California University Berkeley Operations Research Center

Goleman, D. (2014) *Emotional Intelligence.* London: Bloomsbury Publishing.

Institute of Medicine & National Research Council (2015), *Transforming the workforce for children birth through age 8: A unifying foundation.* Washington, DC: National Academies.

McCormick Center for Early Childhood Leadership (2014). *Leadership matters.* Wheeling, IL: National Louis University, McCormick Center for Early Childhood Leadership.

Merriam-Webster Dictionary - retrieved from: https://www.merriam-webster.com/dictionary/competency

Morgan, G. (2000). *The Director is the Key to Quality.* In M. Culkin (Ed.), *Managing Quality in Young Children's Programs: The Leader's Role* (pp. 40-58). New York: Teachers College Press

Wisconsin: Early Learning Standards Steering Committee. (2014). *Model Early Learning Standards: Birth to First Grade, Fourth Edition.* Madison, WI: Wisconsin Department of Public Instruction.

While many state core competency documents were reviewed during the development of the Early Childhood, After School and Youth Development Program Administrator Competencies, the following were particularly important sources of information:

Competencies for Program Directors of Early Childhood and After School Programs, Vermont – retrieved from: http://northernlightscdc.org/wp-content/uploads/2011/07/competencies_program_directors.pdf

Florida Core Competencies for Early Care and Education Directors – retrieved from: https://www.palmbeachstate.edu/ieece/Documents/FLcoreComps-Directors.pdf

Leading Pre-K-3 Learning Communities: Competencies for Effective Principal Practice, Executive Summary – retrieved from: https://www.naesp.org/sites/default/files/leading-pre-k-3-learning-communities-executive-summary.pdf

National Afterschool Association Core Knowledge and Competencies for Afterschool and Youth Development Professionals – retrieved from: http://naaweb.org/resources/core-compentencies

Program Administrator Definition and Competencies, National Association for Education of Young Children – retrieved from: https://www.naeyc.org/academy/files/academy/ProgramAdminDefinitionCompetencies.pdf

Texas Core Competencies for Early Childhood Practitioners and Administrators – retrieved from: https://tecpds.org/Resource/pdf/CoreCompetencies/texascorecompetencies-pract-admin.pdf

Self-Assessment Tool

"The director is the key to quality!" -G. Morgan

The 4 core areas and 14 competencies outlined the scope of the role of an administrator. The intent of this tool is for administrators to use it for self-reflection of daily practice in those 14 competencies. It is NOT intended to be used as an evaluation tool for continued employment. To become the key to increased quality the administrator must continuously assess his/her knowledge, skills and dispositions related to working with children, families and staff. For that reason, we encourage leaders/managers to complete all or parts of this Inventory of Practice that relate specifically to their role. Use it as a tool to determine strengths and to help create a plan for ongoing professional development. We encourage individuals to complete the self-assessment regularly, knowing that each revisit will shed new understanding allowing them to delve deeper into each competency.

"If you're jumping from one situation to the next, when do you have time to re-evaluate who you are as an individual?" – Alex Elle

"Ask yourself if what you're doing today is getting you closer to where you want to be tomorrow." - Radma Verix

"You can't change what's going on around you until you start changing what's going on within you." – Unknown

"It's not what you are that's holding you back. It's what you think you are not." – Anonymous

Scoring Grid – Fill in this bar graph. Remember, the dotted line is to allow you to complete this twice, consider six – twelve months later.

Core Area	Competence	Beginner (1)	Developing (2)	Proficient (3)	Expert (4)
Dispositions	Self-Management				
	Relationship Management				
Operations Management	Compliance with Regulations				
	Business Practices				
	Financial Management and Planning				
	Marketing				
	Human Resources				
Programming for Children and Families	Build Professional Capacity of Workforce				
	Assessment				
	Curriculum Design and Implementation				
	Family and Community Engagement				
Influential Leadership	Inspire a Shared Vision				
	Culture and Climate				
	Advocacy				

Action Plan

And finally, after completing the Inventory of Practice develop a plan for professional growth based on your bar graph. In areas you find yourself an expert, how might you begin to share your expertise with others in the field?

Write one specific goal for yourself. Make sure this goal is achievable and measurable – how will you know when you've accomplished this goal? You might look again at the indicators to write your goal. If you have a long-term goal, something that will take more than a year to complete, consider breaking the goal into smaller, short-term goals that can be accomplished in

3-4 months or less. Then choose one of your short-term goals to complete the Action Plan. Next, break down the goal into steps and complete the grid below.

Example goal: *(Core Area: Programming for Children & Families: Build Professional Capacity of Workforce)*

Long-term goal*: create professional development plans (PDP) with all lead teachers by end of year*

Short-term goal*: develop performance evaluations (PE) for all lead teachers, including PDP goals within 2 months*

STEPS might include*: researching PE articles online; looking over teacher job descriptions; presenting idea at a staff meeting; ask other directors to share their PEs; write first draft; asking a few teachers to review draft once written;*

MY GOAL: (include Core Area Competency, Sub-domain and Competency if helpful)			
CHECK WHEN COMPLETED	STEPS	DUE DATE	RESOURCES NEEDED (website, materials, people, courses, tools, etc.)

What could get in the way of my goal? (check all that apply)

- ☐ Lack of money
- ☐ Lack of time
- ☐ Procrastination
- ☐ Workload
- ☐ Resistance from others
- ☐ No support from others
- ☐ Competing priorities
- ☐ Motivation
- ☐ Not enough knowledge about best practice

- ☐ Getting stuck in the details
- ☐ Fear of failure/success
- ☐ My goal is too big (in this case narrow it down)
- ☐ Avoidance of 'icky' tasks, the ones you don't enjoy
- ☐ Other

_____

How can I overcome the things that might get in my way? (check all that apply)

- ☐ Develop a budget
- ☐ Fundraise
- ☐ Begin saving each month
- ☐ Add STEPS to 'To Do' list
- ☐ Let others know my goal
- ☐ Do a little every day
- ☐ Set aside specific time each week, put it on my calendar

- ☐ Ask for help
- ☐ Present plan to those involved, ask for input
- ☐ Celebrate small successes
- ☐ Complete a time-study, where am I spending my time?
- ☐ Other

_____

Finally, explore resources available to you that address your goal/s. Explore state training calendars, colleges and universities, or local/state/national conferences.

Editor: Angel Stoddard, MS: UW Milwaukee, School of Continuing Education, Center for Early Childhood Professional Development and Leadership

Graphic Artist: Angel Stoddard, MS

Made in the USA
Columbia, SC
14 July 2023